I am a Wolverine

Aaron Carr

LET'S READ
AV²
BY WEIGL™
ADDED VALUE • AUDIO VISUAL

Go to **www.av2books.com**, and enter this book's unique code.

BOOK CODE

N482325

AV² by Weigl brings you media enhanced books that support active learning.

AV² provides enriched content that supplements and complements this book. Weigl's AV² books strive to create inspired learning and engage young minds in a total learning experience.

Your AV² Media Enhanced books come alive with...

Audio
Listen to sections of the book read aloud.

Video
Watch informative video clips.

Embedded Weblinks
Gain additional information for research.

Try This!
Complete activities and hands-on experiments.

Key Words
Study vocabulary, and complete a matching word activity.

Quizzes
Test your knowledge.

Slide Show
View images and captions, and prepare a presentation.

... and much, much more!

Published by AV² by Weigl
350 5th Avenue, 59th Floor   New York, NY   10118
Websites: www.av2books.com   www.weigl.com

Library of Congress Cataloging-in-Publication Data

Carr, Aaron.
 Wolverine / Aaron Carr.
    pages cm. -- (I am)
 ISBN 978-1-4896-2645-5 (hardcover : alk. paper) -- ISBN 978-1-4896-2646-2 (softcover : alk. paper) -- ISBN 978-1-4896-2647-9 (single-user ebk.) -- ISBN 978-1-4896-2648-6 (multi-user ebk.)
 1. Wolverine--Juvenile literature. I. Title.
 QL737.C25C373 2014
 599.76'6--dc23

                           2014038594

Printed in the United States of America in North Mankato, Minnesota
1 2 3 4 5 6 7 8 9 0 18 17 16 15 14

112014
WEP311214

Senior Editor: Heather Kissock   Art Director: Terry Paulhus

Weigl acknowledges Getty Images, iStockphoto, Alamy, and Minden as the primary image suppliers for this title.

I am a Wolverine

In this book, I will teach you about

- myself

- my food

- my home

- my family

and much more!

I am a wolverine.

I live in
cold places.

I leave a strong smell to tell others where I live.

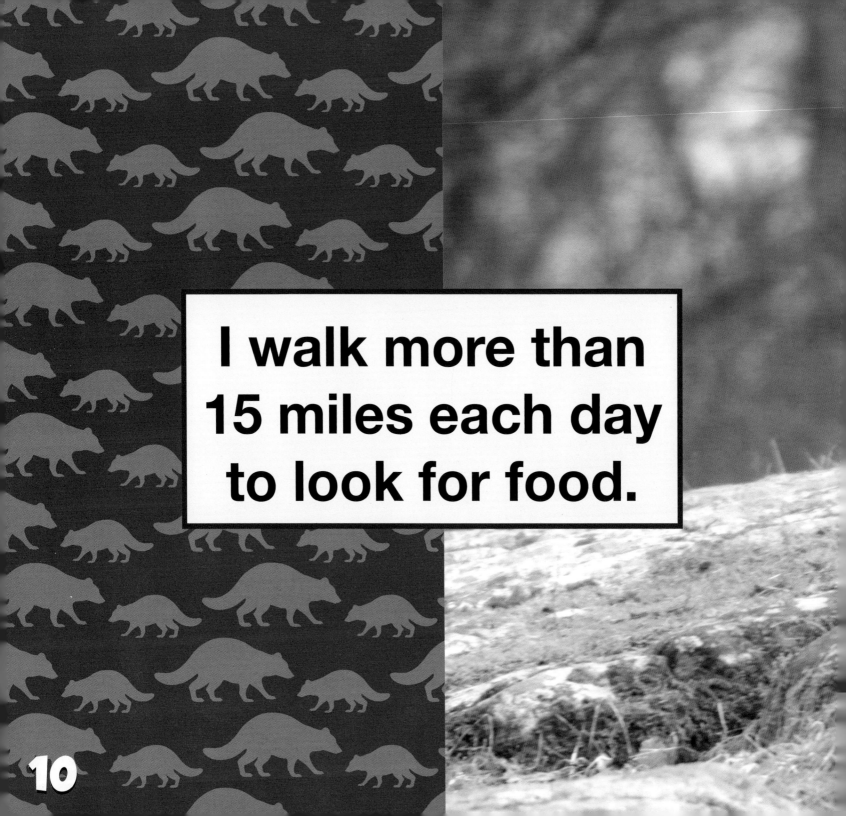

I walk more than 15 miles each day to look for food.

I use the snow as a fridge for my food.

13

I was born
under the snow.

I have fur that keeps the snow away.

16

I have sharp claws to help me climb trees.

18

I need wide spaces to roam.

I am a wolverine.

20

WOLVERINE FACTS

These pages provide detailed information that expands on the interesting facts found in the book. They are intended to be used by adults as a learning support to help young readers round out their knowledge of each amazing animal featured in the *I Am* series.

Pages 4–5

I am a wolverine. Wolverines are the largest members of the weasel family. However, they look more like a small bear than a weasel. Wolverines are known as fierce, strong, and clever animals. A wolverine can be up to 34 inches (86 centimeters) long, not including its 10-inch (26-cm) long tail. It can weigh up to 40 pounds (18 kilograms).

Pages 6–7

I live in cold places. Most wolverines live in cold latitudes, such as the forest and tundra areas of Canada, Alaska, and Russia. A male wolverine will establish a home range of about 580 square miles (1,500 square kilometers). A female's home range is usually about 40 square miles (100 sq. km).

Pages 8–9

I leave a strong smell to tell others where I live. Wolverines are sometimes called skunk bears. This is partly due to their appearance, but also because of the foul-smelling musk they produce. The scent is used mainly in defense when a wolverine is threatened by another animal. Wolverines also use scent to mark their territory.

Pages 10–11

I walk more than 15 miles (24 km) each day to look for food. Wolverines are active animals. They typically walk between 15 and 24 miles (24 and 39 km) each day in the search for food. Wolverines are also known to climb over mountains instead of going around them.

Pages 12–13

I use the snow as a fridge for my food.
Wolverines browse, hunt, and scavenge for their food. They eat plants, rabbits, rodents, and even caribou. Any excess food is stored in the snow, where it stays cool and spoils at a slow pace. A wolverine will return to this food when fresh food sources are scarce.

Pages 14–15

I was born under the snow.
Female wolverines dig a natal den under deep snowpack. This is a safe, hidden place for the kits to be born. Wolverines have between one and five kits at a time. The mother nurses them for 9 to 10 weeks, and they are considered full-grown by seven months. Both parents take turns raising the kits.

Pages 16–17

I have fur that keeps the snow away.
Wolverine fur is thick and covered in natural oils. This makes the fur hydrophobic, which means that it repels snow and frost. Wolverines are able to keep their fur clean and dry in their cold living environment because of this feature.

Pages 18–19

I have sharp claws to help me climb trees.
Wolverines have long, curved claws that can be partly retracted when not in use. They are mostly used for climbing and digging through soil or snowpack. A wolverine's large, furry feet act as snowshoes to help it walk in deep snow.

Pages 20–21

I need wide spaces to roam.
In recent years, human land development has begun to encroach on wolverine habitat. This has reduced the wolverine's range and limited its hunting and scavenging options. Some scientists think wolverines could soon be listed as a vulnerable species as a result.

KEY WORDS

Research has shown that as much as 65 percent of all written material published in English is made up of 300 words. These 300 words cannot be taught using pictures or learned by sounding them out. They must be recognized by sight. This book contains 33 common sight words to help young readers improve their reading fluency and comprehension. This book also teaches young readers several important content words, such as proper nouns. These words are paired with pictures to aid in learning and improve understanding.

Page	Sight Words First Appearance
4	a, am, I
6	in, live, places
8	leave, others, tell, to, where
10	day, each, food, for, look, miles, more, than
12	as, my, the, use
14	under, was
16	away, have, keeps, that
18	help, me, trees
20	need

Page	Content Words First Appearance
4	wolverine
8	smell
12	fridge, snow
14	born
16	fur
18	claws, climb
20	roam, spaces